Fighting for Glory: The History and Legacy of the 54th Massachusetts Volunteer Infantry Regiment

By Charles River Editors

The memorial to Robert Gould Shaw and the 54th on the Boston Common

About Charles River Editors

Introduction

Illustration of the 54th attacking Fort Wagner

The 54th Massachusetts

"A deserted homestead is always a sad sight, but here in the South we must look a little deeper than the surface, and then we see that every such overgrown plantation, and empty house, is a harbinger of freedom to the slaves, and every lover of his country, even if he have no feeling for the slaves themselves, should rejoice." – Robert Gould Shaw

From the Stonewall Brigade to the Iron Brigade, Americans have long been fascinated by the Civil War's most famous and legendary units, and many are familiar with the 20th Maine's defense of Little Round Top at the Battle of Gettysburg. But ironically, perhaps the most famous regiment of the entire war today is the 54th Massachusetts, which was one of the first and ultimately the best known regiment that consisted of black soldiers.

Like most black soldiers, the 54th received discriminatory treatment from the Army, as white men on both sides were wary of trusting black soldiers in heavy combat situations, despite the fact that the 54th acquitted itself well in a nearly suicidal attack at Fort Wagner. As a result, the 54th fought in several battles of lesser note, and they might have faded into obscurity if not for the critically acclaimed movie *Glory*, which looked at the lives of its commander, Colonel Robert Gould Shaw, and its soldiers. Ironically, though it was unknown at the time of the movie, one of the soldiers in the regiment told his captors he had fought for glory.

The movie made the 54th famous, and those who are familiar with the regiment are also familiar with its attack on Fort Wagner, but the story of its creation and its entire service during the Civil War is remarkable from start to finish. The brainchild of abolitionists and the product of a stalled war effort, the 54th was just one of many regiments of black soldiers who fought during the Civil War, and to a large degree it has become representative of the service and sacrifice of black soldiers on behalf of both their country and their civil rights.

Fighting for Glory: The History and Legacy of the 54th Massachusetts comprehensively covers the history and service of the famous regiment in the Civil War, profiling its origins, soldiers, leaders, controversies and legacy. Along with pictures of important people, places, and events, you will learn about the 54th like you never have before, in no time at all.

Chapter 1: Debating the Use of Black Soldiers

"Who would be free themselves must strike the blow....I urge you to fly to arms and smite to death the power that would bury the Government and your liberty in the same hopeless grave. This is your golden opportunity." – Frederick Douglass

After the Battle of Fort Sumter made clear that there would be war between the North and South, support for both the Union and Confederacy rose. Two days after the surrender of the fort, President Abraham Lincoln issued a call-to-arms asking for 75,000 volunteers, a request that would rely on Northern states to organize and train their men.

While most Americans had hoped to avert war, many abolitionists had come to view war as inevitable, and the news from Fort Sumter suggested a chance to rectify the country's original sin through the defeat of the South. Though abolitionists were a minority that was mostly confined to New England and often branded as radicals, they had long sought to end slavery and secure basic civil rights for blacks. One of the most famous abolitionists, the escaped slave Frederick Douglass, realized immediately what kind of opportunity the Civil War presented to all blacks, whether they were slaves or free: "Once let the black man get upon his person the brass letter, U.S., let him get an eagle on his button, and a musket on his shoulder and bullets in his pocket, there is no power on earth that can deny that he has earned the right to citizenship."

Of course, Douglass knew at the time that the Supreme Court's notorious opinion in the *Dred Scott* case had held that no blacks could be citizens, and a federal law dating back to 1792 barred black soldiers from serving in the U.S. Army, even though they had served in the Revolutionary War and the War of 1812 on behalf of both the colonists and British. In 1861, Lincoln was particularly concerned about alienating the border slave states that had not joined the Confederacy, particularly Kentucky and Missouri. The fighting at Fort Sumter had already driven Virginia into the Confederacy, and Lincoln rightly worried that the conscription of black soldiers might alienate whites in the North and the border states. As he famously put it, "I hope to have God on my side, but I must have Kentucky." When Generals John C. Frémont and David Hunter issued proclamations emancipating slaves in their military regions and permitting them to sign up for active duty, the Lincoln Administration swiftly and sternly revoked their orders.

In Boston, Massachusetts, disappointed would-be black volunteers and white supporters met and successfully passed a pro-enlistment resolution that stated, "Our feelings urge us to say to our countrymen that we are ready to stand by and defend our Government as the equals of its white defenders; to do so with our lives, our fortunes, and our sacred honor, for the sake of freedom, and as good citizens; and we ask you to modify your laws, that we may enlist . . . that full scope may be given to the patriotic feelings burning in the colored man's breast."[1]

---

[1] PBS.org website, *Africans in America*, "The Civil War."

Ultimately, and perhaps not surprisingly, the War Department would only change its tune once it felt that doing so was a military necessity. This was a view articulated best by Lincoln himself, who wrote a letter to renowned editor and abolitionist Horace Greeley in August 1862 that stated:

> "I would save the Union. I would save it the shortest way under the Constitution. The sooner the national authority can be restored; the nearer the Union will be 'the Union as it was.' If there be those who would not save the Union, unless they could at the same time save slavery, I do not agree with them. If there be those who would not save the Union unless they could at the same time destroy slavery, I do not agree with them. My paramount object in this struggle is to save the Union, and is not either to save or to destroy slavery. If I could save the Union without freeing any slave I would do it, and if I could save it by freeing all the slaves I would do it; and if I could save it by freeing some and leaving others alone I would also do that. What I do about slavery, and the colored race, I do because I believe it helps to save the Union; and what I forbear, I forbear because I do not believe it would help to save the Union. I shall do less whenever I shall believe what I am doing hurts the cause, and I shall do more whenever I shall believe doing more will help the cause. I shall try to correct errors when shown to be errors; and I shall adopt new views so fast as they shall appear to be true views."

By the time Lincoln had written to Greeley, he had already drafted a preliminary copy of what would become the Emancipation Proclamation. By the summer of 1862, the issue of slavery was intimately connected to the war effort, and it was more important than ever that Lincoln walk a tight line. On one hand, it was important to please the loyal border states where slavery was legal, especially Kentucky and Missouri, but Lincoln also saw the political and military gain that could be had from restricting slavery in the South. In addition to helping stave off foreign intervention by European powers that abhorred slavery, any measure that prevented the Confederates from relying on slaves to power their economy while their white men fought would be a boon for Union arms.

As a hesitant first move, Lincoln signed a bill abolishing slavery in Washington, D.C., in April of 1862, a topic that had been discussed for over a decade. Lincoln supported it during his single term in Congress. With the Southern states not in the fold, there was little controversy over the issue. Most notably, even before Lincoln's letter to Greeley and the issuing of the Emancipation Proclamation, the Union had organized its first black regiment. In July of 1862, General Hunter, the same one whose emancipation order had caused a political crisis in 1861, impressed slaves in the South Carolina Sea Islands and enlisted them in the Union Army to deprive the Confederates of the ability to rely on them.

Hunter

While it was obviously a sensitive issue to emancipate slaves in border states, Lincoln clearly understood the military value gained by adding Southern slaves to the Union war effort, and it was a logical stepping stone from Hunter's actions to simply recruiting blacks to aid the North. On Secretary of State William Seward's advice, Lincoln mulled over the idea of emancipating the slaves – in the Confederacy only – on these grounds. Lincoln could skirt its unconstitutionality by directly making emancipation a war aim, one that could theoretically drain the South of manpower while swelling the Union armies' ranks. At the same time, Lincoln's effective ability to emancipate slaves in the Confederate states was essentially nonexistent; it would require Union armies to advance into Southern soil to free the slaves in that region.

Lincoln thought over the idea for the month, and on July 22, 1862, Lincoln announced to his Cabinet that he planned to free the Confederate slaves, but only after a major Union victory so that the action didn't come across as desperate. The Emancipation Proclamation was born.

Lincoln would have his moment to announce the Emancipation Proclamation in September. Ironically, the bloodiest day in American history took place on the 75th anniversary of the signing of the Constitution. On September 17, 1862, Robert E. Lee's Confederate Army of Northern Virginia fought George McClellan's Union Army of the Potomac outside Sharpsburg along Antietam Creek. That day, nearly 25,000 would become casualties, and Lee's army barely survived fighting the much bigger Northern army. Although the battle was tactically a draw, it resulted in forcing Lee's army out of Maryland and back into Virginia, making it a strategic victory for the North and an opportune time for President Lincoln to issue the Emancipation Proclamation. Five days later, Lincoln announced to the world that on January 1st, 1863, the Emancipation Proclamation would go into effect. Rebellious states were given 100 days to rejoin the Union, at which point they would not necessarily lose ownership of their slaves.

The Emancipation Proclamation also factored prominently into American foreign policy. France and Great Britain were flirting with the idea of diplomatically acknowledging the Confederacy, and Great Britain in particular relied heavily on Southern cotton for its textile industry. However, the Proclamation and Battle of Antietam convinced them otherwise. Neither nation was particularly interested in getting involved militarily with the war, and Antietam threw the Confederacy's favorable military position into question.

The Battle of Antietam and its result, the Emancipation Proclamation, marked a major turning point in the Civil War, but that was unclear in September 1862. At the time, Lincoln was actually disappointed, despite having forced the Confederates out of Maryland. Though the Army of the Potomac was victorious in the Maryland Campaign, Lincoln was disenchanted with McClellan's inability to pursue Lee's army further, thinking he had missed a chance to deliver a knockout punch against Lee. Lincoln would replace McClellan with General Ambrose Burnside, and it was made clear to Burnside that offensive operations against Lee's army were expected immediately.

Through a mix of logistical complications and general incompetence, Burnside suffered a debacle at the Battle of Fredericksburg in December 1862, closing the year on a low note in the Eastern theater of the war. Naturally, Fredericksburg represented one of the low points of the Civil War for the North, and Lincoln reacted to the news by writing, "If there is a worse place than hell, I am in it." It showed too, as noted by Pennsylvania Governor Andrew Curtin, who told Lincoln after touring the battlefield, "It was not a battle, it was a butchery". Curtin noted the president was "heart-broken at the recital, and soon reached a state of nervous excitement bordering on insanity." Radical Republicans frustrated at the prosecution of the war took it out on the generals and the Lincoln Administration; Michigan Senator Zachariah Chandler claimed, "The President is a weak man, too weak for the occasion, and those fool or traitor generals are wasting time and yet more precious blood in indecisive battles and delays."

At the same time, the decisive Confederate victory buoyed the Confederacy's hopes. Confederate commander Robert E. Lee was described by the *Charleston Mercury* as "jubilant, almost off-balance, and seemingly desirous of embracing everyone who calls on him." The results of Antietam and the Maryland Campaign from 3 months earlier were apparently old news or forgotten by the *Mercury*, which boasted, "General Lee knows his business and the army has yet known no such word as fail."

It was in the midst of these events that the Lincoln Administration and the War Department shifted course and began to concentrate on actually utilizing all the available manpower at their disposal, including free blacks in the North who wanted to fight for their country, abolition, and civil rights, and Confederate slaves who were all too happy to escape slavery. Luis Emilio, one of the original officers of the 54th Massachusetts and the author of *A Brave Black regiment: The History of the 54th Regiment of Massachusetts Volunteer Infantry, 1863-1865*, noted the military and political situation at the close of 1862:

"At the close of the year 1862, the military situation was discouraging to the supporters of the Federal Government. We had been repulsed at Fredericksburg and at Vicksburg, and at tremendous cost had fought the battle of Stone River. Some sixty-five thousand troops would be discharged during the ensuing summer and fall. Volunteering was at a standstill. On the other hand, the Confederates, having filled their ranks, were never better fitted for conflict. Politically, the opposition had grown formidable, while the so-called 'peace-faction' was strong, and active for mediation."

Emilio

Although there was jubilant talk in the South of the North giving up the fight imminently after Fredericksburg, it was clearly premature, and to a degree Emilio's analysis overstated the trouble the North was in. Lee had concluded an incredibly successful year for the Confederates in the East, but the South was still struggling. The Confederate forces in the West had failed to win a major battle, suffering defeat at places like Shiloh in Tennessee and across the Mississippi River, and as the war continued into 1863, the Southern economy continued to deteriorate. Southern armies were suffering serious deficiencies of nearly all supplies as the Union blockade continued to be effective at stopping most international commerce with the Confederacy. Moreover, the prospect of Great Britain or France recognizing the Confederacy had been all but eliminated by the Emancipation Proclamation. Given the unlikelihood of forcing the North's capitulation, the Confederacy's main hope for victory was to win some decisive victory or hope that Abraham Lincoln would lose his reelection bid in 1864, and that the new president would want to negotiate peace with the Confederacy.

Chapter 2: Organizing the 54th Massachusetts

By the end of 1862, a couple of all-black units had been informally raised and organized. In addition to General Hunter's actions in South Carolina, General Benjamin Butler organized the Louisiana Native Guards out of free blacks while he was the governor of Union-occupied New Orleans. Meanwhile, in October 1862 General Rufus Saxton organized the 1st South Carolina regiment out of "contrabands", the word used by Northerners to refer to escaped slaves , in the Department of the South, formed the First South Carolina from contrabands in October of the same year. In Kansas, Colonel James Williams organized the First Kansas Colored unit in the summer of 1862.

On January 1, 1863, the Emancipation Proclamation officially went into effect, proclaiming the freedom of over three million slaves in the Confederate states currently in rebellion. While it was understood that the Emancipation Proclamation was essentially powerless to compel abolition in the Confederacy, it did affect those slaves that could reach the lines of the Union armies. As a result, the Proclamation immediately freed 50,000 slaves, while holding out the promise of freeing the rest as Union armies advanced.

Meanwhile, Secretary of War Edwin Stanton began implementing the policies that would allow the North to formally organize and train black soldiers. Naturally, that effort started with Massachusetts, where Governor John A. Andrew was an outspoken critic of slavery. In 1862, the governor advocated the recruitment of black soldiers and had worked with Frederick Douglass to try to convince other Northern governors to support that stance. During the war years, he famously commented, "I know not what record of sin awaits me in the other world, but this I know, that I was never mean enough to despise any man because he was black."

Governor Andrew

Given his advocacy, it was only fitting that Governor Andrew received the initial order to raise a black regiment. On January 20, 1863, Andrew was order

"War Department, Washington City, Jan. 20, 1863.

Ordered: That Governor Andrew of Massachusetts is authorized, until further orders, to raise such number of volunteers, companies of artillery for duty in the forts of Massachusetts and elsewhere, and such corps of infantry for the volunteer military service as he may find convenient, such volunteers to be enlisted for three years, or until sooner discharged, and may include persons of African descent, organized into special corps. He will make the usual needful requisitions on the appropriate staff bureaus and officers, for the proper transportation, organization, supplies, subsistence, arms and equipments of such volunteers.

Edwin M. Stanton, Secretary of War."

Once Andrew had been granted the ability to organize black regiments, he immediately turned to filling its leadership positions, something he had clearly been considering for awhile. A week after Stanton's order, Andrew wrote a letter to Francis Shaw in which he explained who he had in mind to lead the 54th Massachusetts:

"Boston, Jan. 30, 1863.

Francis G. Shaw, Esq., Staten Island, N. Y.

Dear sir,—As you may have seen by the newspapers, I am about to raise a colored regiment in Massachusetts. This I cannot but regard as perhaps the most important corps to be organized during the whole war, in view of what must be the composition of our new levies; and therefore I am very anxious to organize it judiciously, in order that it may be a model for all future colored regiments. I am desirous to have for its officers —particularly for its field-officers—young men of military experience, of firm antislavery principles, ambitious, superior to a vulgar contempt for color, and having faith in the capacity of colored men for military service. Such officers must necessarily be gentlemen of the highest tone and honor; and I shall look for them in those circles of educated antislavery society which, next to the colored race itself, have the greatest interest in this experiment.

Reviewing the young men of the character I have described, now in the Massachusetts service, it occurs to me to offer the colonelcy to your son, Captain Shaw, of the Second Massachusetts Infantry, and the lieutenant-colonelcy to Captain Hallowell of the Twentieth Massachusetts Infantry, the son of Mr. Morris L. Hallowell of Philadelphia. With my deep conviction of the importance of this undertaking, in view of the fact that it will be the first colored regiment to be raised in the free States, and that its success or its failure will go far to elevate or depress the estimation in which the character of the colored Americans will be held throughout the world, the command of such a regiment seems to me to be a high object of ambition for any officer. How much your son may have reflected upon such a subject I do not know, nor have I any information of his disposition for such a task except what I have derived from his general character and reputation; nor should I wish him to undertake it unless he could enter upon it with a full sense of its importance, with an earnest determination for its success, and with the assent and sympathy and support of the opinions of his immediate family.

I therefore enclose you the letter in which I make him the offer of this commission; and I will be obliged to you if you will forward it to him, accompanying it with any expression to him of your own views, and if you will also write to me upon the subject. My mind is drawn towards Captain Shaw by many considerations. I am sure he would attract the support, sympathy, and active co-operation of many among his immediate family relatives. The more ardent, faithful, and true Republicans and friends of liberty would recognize in him a scion from a tree whose fruit and leaves have always contributed to the strength and healing of our generation. So it is with Captain Hallowell. His father is a Quaker gentleman of Philadelphia, two of whose sons are officers in our army, and another is a merchant in Boston. Their house in Philadelphia is a hospital and home for Massachusetts officers; and the family are full of good works; and he was the adviser and confidant of our soldiery when sick or on duty in that city. I need not add that young Captain Hallowell is a gallant and fine fellow, true as steel to the cause of humanity, as well as to the flag of the country."

Robert Gould Shaw was a battle-hardened veteran by January 1863, having served in the 7th New York and the 2nd Massachusetts Shaw, and he had fought at Antietam, earning a promotion to the rank of Captain. Emilio described the man destined to lead the 54th, "Colonel Shaw was of medium height, with light hair and fair complexion, of pleasing aspect and composed in his manners. His bearing was graceful, as became a soldier and gentleman. His family connections were of the highest social standing, character, and influence."

The Shaws were well-known abolitionists, and Andrew had written to Robert's father out of fear that Robert might have declined the offer if Andrew wrote to him. Sure enough, when Francis personally delivered Andrew's offer to his son on February 3, he found his son reluctant to lead the "special corps" that Andrew intended to organize. After initially saying no, Robert ultimately agreed a couple of days later, in order to please his father.

Robert Gould Shaw

With Captain Shaw in place as the leader, there were still other leadership positions to fill, and Emilio described the process of recruitment:

> "Line-officers were commissioned from persons nominated by commanders of regiments in the field, by tried friends of the movement, the field-officers, and those Governor Andrew personally desired to appoint. This freedom of selection,— unhampered by claims arising from recruits furnished or preferences of the enlisted men, so powerful in officering white regiments,—secured for this organization a corps of officers who brought exceptional character, experience, and ardor to their allotted work. Of the twenty-nine who took the field, fourteen were veteran soldiers from three-years regiments, nine from nine-months regiments, and one from the militia; six had previously been commissioned. They included representatives of well-known families; several were Harvard men; and some, descendants of officers of the Revolution and the War of 1812. Their average age was about twenty-three years.
>
> At the time a strong prejudice existed against arming the blacks and those who dared to command them. The sentiment of the country and of the army was opposed to the measure. It was asserted that they would not fight, that their employment would prolong the war, and that white troops would refuse to serve with them. Besides the moral courage required to accept commissions in the 54th at the time it was organizing…"

What Emilio did not mention is that all the commissioned officers of the regiment would be white. In an effort to make black enlistment more palatable to the Northern public, and to placate the racist elements within the Army, the War Department decreed that "colored" soldiers would serve exclusively in strictly segregated units. Subsequently, Lieutenant Colonel Norwood P. Hallowell was commissioned colonel of the newly-forming 54th, but he would be almost immediately replaced by his brother, Major Edward "Ned" Needles Hallowell. Edward was the first white officer to occupy the barracks designated for the 54th at Camp Meigs, and he was so successful at recruiting black soldiers in Philadelphia that he was responsible for prompting the formation of the 55th Massachusetts. Norwood would be put in command of the 55th, and Edward would thus be promoted to major and made second-in-command under Captain Shaw.

Shaw was an avid abolitionist who fully believed in the cause, but he was reluctant to lead a black regiment because he was fully aware that it would tarnish his reputation among many in the North. In addition to simple racism, whites on both sides widely believed that black soldiers could not be relied on, not only because they were perceived to be inferior but also because their loyalty to the cause had to be questioned. Southerners were understandably wary about arming slaves in the presence of their masters, while Northerners had to wonder whether blacks would fight hard for a country that had discriminated against them throughout its entire existence. Governor Andrew himself held similar prejudices, noting to a friend that the black soldiers would be kept disciplined because they "shall be commanded by officers who are eminently gentlemen."

Furthermore, the Confederacy sought to intimidate black soldiers and those who would command them, in an effort to discourage the use of this new influx of manpower. On May 1, 1863, the Confederate Congress passed legislation that read:

"Section IV: That every white person being a commissioned officer, or acting as such, who, during the present war, shall command negroes or mulattoes in arms against the Confederate States, or who shall arm, train, organize, or prepare negroes or mulattoes for military service against the Confederate States, or who shall voluntarily aid negroes or mulattoes in any military enterprise, attack, or conflict in such service, shall be deemed as inciting servile insurrection, and shall, if captured, be put to death or be otherwise punished at the discretion of the Court."

William Simpkins, a white officer in the 54th who would die in the assault on Fort Wagner, noted the dangers in a letter to his family, writing,

"I have to tell you of a pretty important step that I have just taken. I have given my name to be forwarded to Massachusetts for a commission in the 54th Negro Regiment, Colonel Shaw. This is no hasty conclusion, no blind leap of an enthusiast, but the result of much hard thinking. It will not be at first, and probably not for a long time, an agreeable position, for many reasons too evident to state. . . . Then this is nothing but an experiment after all; but it is an experiment that I think it high time we should try,—an experiment which, the sooner we prove fortunate the sooner we can count upon an immense number of hardy troops that can stand the effect of a Southern climate without injury; an experiment which the sooner we prove unsuccessful, the sooner we shall establish an important truth and rid ourselves of a false hope."

At the same time, blacks in Massachusetts who were eager to fight flocked in from all parts of the state to join the regiment. Among the first to answer the call of duty was James "Henry" Gooding, one of 53 Black recruits from New Bedford, Massachusetts. Gooding was a successful twenty-five-year-old sea cook who wrote to a relative shortly before he joined the Union Army, "Our people must know that if they are ever to attain to any position in the eyes of the civilized world, they must forgo comfort, home, fear, and above all, superstition, and fight for it. They must learn that there is more dignity in carrying a musket in defense of liberty and right than there is in shaving a man's face or waiting on somebody's table."[2]

There was also plenty of efforts made by Andrew and other state officials to go about finding and recruiting the manpower to form the 54th Massachusetts. Emilio explained:

---

[2]   Stevens, Joseph E. *1863: The Rebirth of a Nation*. Page 112.

Much the larger number of recruits were obtained through the organization and by the means which will now be described. About February 15, Governor Andrew appointed a committee to superintend the raising of recruits for the colored regiment, consisting of George L. Stearns, Amos A. Lawrence, John M. Forbes, William I. Bowditch, Le Baron Russell, and Richard P. Hallowell, of Boston; Mayor Howland and James B. Congdon, of New Bedford; Willard P. Phillips, of Salem; and Francis G. Shaw, of New York. Subsequently the membership was increased to one hundred, and it became known as the 'Black Committee.' It was mainly instrumental in procuring the men of the 54th and Fifty-fifth Massachusetts Infantry, the Fifth Massachusetts Cavalry, besides 3,967 other colored men credited to the State. All the gentlemen named were persons of prominence. Most of them had been for years in the van of those advanced thinkers and workers who had striven to help and free the slave wherever found.

The first work of this committee was to collect money; and in a very short time five thousand dollars was received, Gerrit Smith, of New York, sending his check for five hundred dollars. Altogether nearly one hundred thousand dollars was collected, which passed through the hands of Richard P. Hallowell, the treasurer, who was a brother of the Hallowells commissioned in the 54th. A call for recruits was published in a hundred journals from east to west. Friends whose views were known were communicated with, and their aid solicited; but the response was not for a time encouraging

With the need came the man."

Shortly after Massachusetts announced that it had met its minimum quota, Michigan, Illinois, Indiana, Ohio, Pennsylvania, New York, Connecticut, and Rhode Island all formed their own all-Black units. Receiving considerable moral support from abolitionists in Massachusetts, including American essayist, lecturer, poet, and leader of the Transcendentalist movement, Ralph Waldo Emerson, the 54th Massachusetts became the object of great interest and curiosity due to its position as one of the first black units formally organized in the North. Many would view its performance as indicative of whether black soldiers would be the equal of white soldiers.

Chapter 3: Training the 54th Massachusetts

In late March 1863, Governor Andrew sought to assure abolitionist George T. Downing that black soldiers would be treated fairly, writing to him:

"Dear sir,—In reply to your inquiries made as to the position of colored men who may be enlisted into the volunteer service of the United States, I would say that their position in respect to pay, equipments, bounty, or any aid or protection when so mustered is that of any and all other volunteers.

I desire further to state to you that when I was in Washington on one occasion, in an interview with Mr. Stanton, the Secretary of War, he stated in the most emphatic manner that he would never consent that free colored men should be accepted into the service to serve as soldiers in the South, until he should be assured that the Government of the United States was prepared to guarantee and defend to the last dollar and the last man, to these men, all the rights, privileges, and immunities that are given by the laws of civilized warfare to other soldiers. Their present acceptance and muster — in as soldiers pledges the honor of the nation in the same degree and to the same rights with all. They will be soldiers of the Union, nothing less and nothing different. I believe they will earn for themselves an honorable fame, vindicating their race and redressing their future from the aspersions of the past."

Andrew's promises would go unfulfilled. Once the regiment had been organized, the 54th was sent to train at Camp Meigs in Readville, near Boston. The poor and unequal treatment that would plague the 54th throughout the war started with its training post, a miserable facility described as "a collection of crudely-constructed buildings sitting in a sea of icy mud [inside which] were tiers of coffin-shaped sleeping bunks lining windowless walls."[3] Emilio would similarly describe the camp: "The ground was flat, and well adapted for drilling, but in wet weather was muddy, and in the winter season bleak and cheerless. The barracks were great barn-like structures of wood with sleeping-bunks on either side." The regiment was immediately provided warm clothes and military essentials to brave the cold weather and inhospitable surroundings. ,

Furthermore, as it became evident that many more recruits were coming forward than anticipated, the medical exam for the 54th became what was described by the Massachusetts Surgeon-General as "rigid and thorough". The result was what many historians characterize as the most "robust, strong, and healthy set of men" ever mustered into military service in the United States. Among its recruits were Lewis N. and Charles Douglass, sons of abolitionist Frederick Douglass, who had worked so tirelessly that he personally provided the initial recruitment effort with 100 black recruits.

Over the next few months, more and more recruits made their way to Camp Meigs, and Emilio noted the high morale:

"From the outset, the regiment showed great interest in drilling, and on guard duty it was always vigilant and active. The barracks, cook-houses, and kitchens far surpassed in cleanliness any I have ever witnessed, and were models of neatness and good order. The cooks, however, had many of them been in similar employment in other places, and had therefore brought some skill to the present responsibility.

In camp, these soldiers presented a buoyant cheerfulness and hilarity, which impressed me with the idea that the monotony of their ordinary duties would not ~~dampen their feeling of cont~~entment, if they were well cared for. On parade, their

[3] Stevens, Joseph E. *1863: The Rebirth of a Nation.* Page 114.

appearance was marked with great neatness of personal appearance as concerned dress and the good condition in which their arms and accoutrements were kept. Their habits being imitative, it was natural that they should be punctilious in matters of military etiquette, and such observances as the well disciplined soldier, in his subordinate position, pays to his superior. And fortunately for them, they had the teachings of those who were not only thoroughly imbued with the importance of their trusts, but were gentlemen as well as soldiers.

It was remarked that there was less drunkenness in this regiment than in any that had ever left Massachusetts; but this may have been owing to the fact that the bounty was not paid them until a day or two previous to their departure."

Those sentiments were also echoed by Shaw, who reported that he was impressed with how well the recruits were doing in camp: "If the success of the Fifty-fourth gives you so much pleasure, I shall have no difficulty in giving you good words of it whenever I write. Everything goes on prosperously. The intelligence of the men is a great surprise to me. They learn all the details of guard duty and camp service infinitely more readily than most of the Irish I have had under my command. There is not the least doubt that we shall leave the State with as good a regiment as any that has marched."

By the end of May, the 54th was ready for combat. After several weeks of rigorous training, during which the members of the 54th were tested to make sure they could perform in a variety of complex small-unit and large-unit maneuvers under fire, on May 18, 1863, several thousand spectators gathered for the official presentation of the regional, state, and national colors. This momentous event, which drew statesmen and other prominent figures, as well as reporters from neighboring states, marked the end of the unit's training period and the beginning of its official service to the United States Union Army.

Near the end of the ceremony, Governor Andrew addressed the regiment, and specifically Robert Gould Shaw:

"To those men of Massachusetts and of surrounding States who have now made themselves citizens of Massachusetts, I have no word to utter fit to express the emotions of my heart. These men, sir, have now, in the Providence of God, given to them an opportunity which, while it is personal to themselves, is still an opportunity for a whole race of men. With arms possessed of might to strike a blow, they have found breathed into their hearts an inspiration of devoted patriotism and regard for their brethren of their own color, which has inspired them with a purpose to nerve that arm, that it may strike a blow which, while it shall help to raise aloft their country's flag— their country's flag, now, as well as ours—by striking down the foes which oppose it, strikes also the last shackle which binds the limbs of the bondmen in the Rebel States.

I know not, Mr. Commander, when, in all human history, to any given thousand men in arms there has been committed a work at once so proud, so precious, so full of hope and glory as the work committed to you. And may the infinite mercy of Almighty God attend you every hour of every day through all the experiences and vicissitudes of that dangerous life in which you have embarked; may the God of our fathers cover your heads in the day of battle; may He shield you with the arms of everlasting power; may He hold you always—most of all, first of all, and last of all—up to the highest and holiest conception of duty, so that if, on the field of stricken fight, your souls shall be delivered from the thralldom of the flesh, your spirits shall go home to God, bearing aloft the exulting thought of duty well performed, of glory and reward won, even at the hands of the angels who shall watch over you from above!

Mr. Commander, you, sir, and most of your officers, have been carefully selected from among the most intelligent and experienced officers who have already performed illustrious service upon the field during the two years of our national conflict. I need not say, sir, with how much confidence and with how much pride we contemplate the leadership which this regiment will receive at your hands. In yourself, sir, your staff and line officers, we are enabled to declare a confidence which knows no hesitation and no doubt. Whatever fortune may betide you, we know from the past that all will be done for the honor of the cause, for the protection of the flag, for the defence of the right, for the glory of your country, and for the safety and the honor of these men whom we commit to you, that shall lie either in the human heart, or brain, or arm.

And now, Mr. Commander, it is my most agreeable duty and high honor to hand to you, as the representative of the Fifty-fourth Regiment of Massachusetts Volunteers, the American flag, 'the star-spangled banner' of the Republic. Wherever its folds shall be unfurled, it will mark the path of glory. Let its stars be the inspiration of yourself, your officers, and your men. As the gift of the young ladies of the city of Boston to their brethren in arms, they will cherish it as the lover cherishes the recollection and fondness of his mistress; and the white stripes of its field will be red with their blood before it shall be surrendered to the foe."

At the close of Andrew's remarks, Shaw responded:

"Your Excellency: We accept these flags with feelings of deep gratitude. They will remind us not only of the cause we are fighting for, and of our country, but of the friends we have left behind us, who have thus far taken so much interest in this regiment, and whom we know will follow us in our career. Though the greater number of men in this regiment are not Massachusetts men, I know there is not one who will not be proud to fight and serve under our flag. May we have an opportunity to show that you have not made a mistake in intrusting the honor of the State to a colored regiment,—the first State that has sent one to the war."

10 days later, on May 28, the 54th Massachusetts Volunteer Infantry Regiment was sent off to the South. After traveling by rail from Readville to Boston, they headed to Battery Wharf and boarded the steamer *DeMolay*, waiting to transport them to the Sea Islands, South Carolina. Even this was a spectacle, and one publication of the day reported, "Vast crowds lined the streets where the regiment was to pass, and the Common was crowded with an immense number of people such as only the Fourth of July or some rare event causes to assemble. . . . No white regiment from Massachusetts has surpassed the Fifty-fourth in excellence of drill, while in general discipline, dignity, and military bearing the regiment is acknowledged by every candid mind to be all that can be desired."

Unbeknownst to the soldiers, as well as the hundreds of people who came out to see them off and wish them well, the police had backups ready to quell any riots just in case there were disturbances.

Chapter 4: Joining the Fight

Shortly after arriving at Hilton Head, South Carolina on June 3, 1863, the regiment was immediately put to manual labor, hardly what Shaw or his soldiers had in mind when they were drilling at Camp Meigs. Emilio described the first few days, writing, "While camped there, the days were intensely hot, with cooler nights. Troublesome insects infested our camp. Shelter tents for the men were issued and put up. Our first taste of fatigue work in the field was on June 6, when Companies A, D, and H were sent out on the shell road to work on fortifications. The Second South Carolina had departed for the Georgia coast. Late in the day orders came to embark, Colonel Shaw having applied for active service."

The 54th would be ordered into a fight of sorts, but it certainly wasn't the kind of fighting it had in mind. On June 11, the 54th took part in a raid on the town of Darien, Georgia that was ordered by Colonel James Montgomery, an ardent abolitionist who commanded the Second South Carolina Volunteers. Given the opportunity to take the fight to the South, Montgomery was only too happy to loot and burn the town. One officer of the 54th described the scene as Union soldiers entered Darien:

'The men began to come in by twos, threes, and dozens, loaded with every species and all sorts and quantities of furniture, stores, trinkets, etc., till one would be tired enumerating. We had sofas, tables, pianos, chairs, mirrors, carpets, beds, bedsteads, carpenter's tools, cooper's tools, books, law-books, account-books in unlimited supply, china sets, tinware, earthenware, Confederate shinplasters, old letters, papers, etc. A private would come along with a slate, yard-stick, and a brace of chickens in one hand, and in the other hand a rope with a cow attached.'

The 54th's participation in the raid was minimal, however, because the reluctant Colonel Shaw initially objected to what he called a "satanic action". Only one company of the 54th would participate in the action, and Shaw himself reported on the vandalism wreaked by Montgomery's men:

> "After the town was pretty thoroughly disembowelled, [Montgomery] said to me, 'I shall burn this town.' He speaks in a very low tone, and has quite a sweet smile when addressing you. I told him I did not want the responsibility of it, and he was only too happy to take it all on his own shoulders. . . . The reasons he gave me for destroying Darien were that the Southerners must be made to feel that this was a real war, and that they were to be swept away by the hand of God like the Jews of old. In theory it may seem all right to some; but when it comes to being made the instrument of the Lord's vengeance, I myself don't like it. Then he says, 'We are outlawed, and therefore not bound by the rules of regular warfare.' But that makes it none the less revolting to wreak our vengeance on the innocent and defenceless."

In fact, Shaw was so shocked by Montgomery's men burning down almost all of Darien that he wrote a letter to the officers of the X Corps asking if the actions had been sanctioned by General Hunter:

> "Dear sir,—Will you allow me to ask you a private question, which of course you are at liberty to answer or not? Has Colonel Montgomery orders from General Hunter to burn and destroy all town and dwelling houses he may capture?

> On the 11th inst., as you know, we took the town of Darien without opposition, the place being occupied, as far as we ascertained, by non-combatants; Colonel Montgomery burned it to the ground, and at leaving finally, shelled it from the river.

> If he does this on his own responsibility, I shall refuse to have a share in it, and take the consequences; but, of course, if it is an order from headquarters, it is a different matter, as in that case I suppose it to have been found necessary to adopt that policy. He ordered me, if separated from him, to burn all the plantation houses I came across.

> Now, I am perfectly ready to burn any place which resists, and gives some reason for such a proceeding; but it seems to me barbarous to turn women and children adrift in that way; and if I am only assisting Colonel Montgomery in a private enterprise of his own, it is very distasteful to me.

> I am aware that this is not a military way of getting information; and I hope you will feel that I shall not be hurt if you refuse to answer my question."

No doubt to his surprise, Shaw learned that Montgomery had indeed acted pursuant to Hunter's orders and wishes.

This action was followed on June 16 by their participation in the failed Union attempt to capture Charleston, South Carolina, during which the 54th Massachusetts effectively stopped a Confederate assault near James Island and lost 42 men in the process. By the end of June, they were stationed back near Hilton Head.

Initially, Colonel Shaw was at first quite unhappy with his soldiers and referred to them in derogatory terms to his superiors, but by July, he had recanted that assessment and reported that he was perfectly astonished at the general intelligence…They learn all the details of guard duty and camp service infinitely more readily than most of the Irish I have had under my command!" After seeing the determination and bravery of his men, he personally stopped referring to them in derogatory terms and epithets to fellow officers, and he began vehemently defending them against critics from the Union Army and members of the press.

As the 54th was performing its initial service in the war, following the Siege of Port Hudson, which lasted from May 21-July 9, Union Major General Nathaniel P. Banks provided black soldiers their first major endorsement, saying, "Whatever any doubts may have existed heretofore as to the efficiency of Negro regiments, the history on this day proves conclusively to those who were in condition to observe the conduct of this regiment that the government will find in this class of troops effective supporters and defenders. The severe test to which they were subjected, and the determined manner in which they encountered the enemy, leaves upon my mind no doubt of their ultimate success."[4]

Nevertheless, Shaw had to deal with troublesome rumors and problems regarding potential discrimination against his men. On June 30, as the 54th was mustered to receive its pay, rumors spread that they would not be getting paid what they were promised, prompting Shaw to write to Governor Andrew on July 2:

"dear sir,—Since I last wrote you, the Fifty-fourth has left St. Simon's Island and returned to St. Helena near Hilton Head. We are now encamped in a healthy place, close to the harbor, where we get the sea breeze.

You have probably seen the order from Washington which cuts down the pay of colored troops from $13 to $10. Of course if this affects Massachusetts regiments, it will be a great piece of injustice to them, as they were enlisted on the express understanding that they were to be on precisely the same footing as all other Massachusetts troops. In my opinion they should be mustered out of the service or receive the full pay which was promised them. The paymaster here is inclined to class us with the contraband regiments, and pay the men only $10. If he does not change his mind, I shall refuse to have the regiment paid until I hear from you on the subject. And at any rate I trust you will take the matter in hand, for every pay-day we shall have the same trouble unless there is a special order to prevent it.

4   Lanning, Michael. *The Civil War 100*. Page 143.

Another change that has been spoken of was the arming of negro troops with pikes instead of firearms. Whoever proposed it must have been looking for a means of annihilating negro troops altogether, I should think—or have never been under a heavy musketry fire, nor observed its effects. The project is now abandoned, I believe.

My men are well and in good spirits. We have only five in hospital. We are encamped near the Second South Carolina near General Strong's brigade, and are under his immediate command. He seems anxious to do all he can for us, and if there is a fight in the Department will no doubt give the black troops a chance to show what stuff they are made of.

With many wishes for your good health and happiness, I remain,

Very sincerely and respectfully yours,

Robert G. Shaw."

In addition to being treated unfairly when it came to pay, Shaw was also upset at what he perceived to be a reluctance by his superiors to use the 54th in active combat operations. On July 6, he wrote to the regiment's Brigadier-General, George C. Strong:

"General,—I did not pay my respects to you before you left this post because I did not wish to disturb you when making your preparations for departure.

I desire, however, to express to you my regret that my regiment no longer forms a part of the force under your command. I was the more disappointed at being left behind, that I had been given to understand that we were to have our share in the work in this department. I feel convinced too that my men are capable of better service than mere guerilla warfare, and I hoped to remain permanently under your command.

It seems to me quite important that the colored soldiers should be associated as much as possible with the white troops, in order that they may have other witnesses besides their own officers to what they are capable of doing. I trust that the present arrangement is not permanent.

With many wishes for your success, believe me very sincerely and respectfully

Your obedient servant,

Robert G. Shaw, Colonel Commanding Fifty-fourth Regiment Mass. Infantry."

As it turned out, the 54th would get its chance less than two weeks later.

Chapter 5: Fort Wagner

On July 8, the 54th was transported to Folly Island, an island surrounding Morris Island, one of the islands defended by Confederates near the entrance to Charleston's harbor. The Union was conducting operations in 1863 in an attempt to capture that critical Southern city and its harbor, which had been the site of the Battle of Fort Sumter back in April 1861. Morris Island was one of the outermost islands in Charleston's harbor and was thus crucial for the Confederates to hold, so that blockade runners could safely leave Charleston's ports. It also made for a tempting and necessary target for the Union, who hoped to capture Morris Island and then place its own batteries there to fire at forts that ringed the inner harbor, including Fort Sumter.

The problem for the North was that Morris Island was guarded by Fort Wagner, one of the most intimidating Confederate forts on the Eastern seaboard. Fort Wagner was heavily protected from any potential naval attacks, but at the same time it could only be assaulted on land in one direction because the fort spanned from the Atlantic to swamp water that could not be marched through. Since the location necessarily channeled any infantry attack toward a certain part of the wall, the wall rose as high as 30 feet in some places, and a deep trench of water was placed in its front, along with buried land mines and abatis in the form of palmetto stakes.

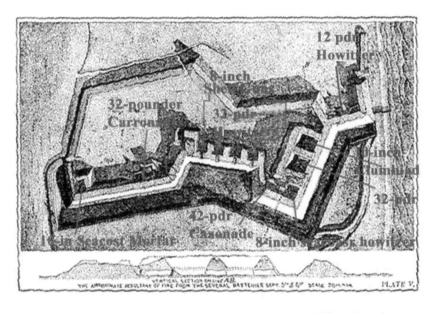

A model of Fort Wagner and its artillery defenses from the Official Records.

The natural defenses of the structure were impressive enough, but the fort's artillery also included one 10-inch seacoast mortar, two 32 lb. carronades, two 8-inch shell guns, two 32 lb. howitzers, a 42 lb. carronade, and an 8-inch seacoast mortar on the land face. The fort's garrison also consisted of the 1st South Carolina Artillery, the Charleston Battalion, the 31st North Carolina, and the 51st North Carolina.

On July 11, a week before the 54th's legendary assault on Fort Wagner, a substantial attack was made on Fort Wagner by Union soldiers from George Strong's brigade, under the orders of department commander Brigadier General Quincy Adams Gillmore. Emilio explained the plan for Gillmore's attack:

"He desired to gain possession of Morris Island, then in the enemy's hands, and fortified. He had at disposal ten thousand infantry, three hundred and fifty artillerists, and six hundred engineers; thirty-six pieces of field artillery, thirty Parrott guns, twenty-seven siege and three Cohorn mortars, besides ample tools and material. Admiral Dahlgren was to co-operate. On Folly Island, in our possession, batteries were constructed near Lighthouse Inlet, opposite Morris Island, concealed by the sand hillocks and undergrowth. Gillmore's real attack was to be made from this point by a coup de main, the infantry crossing the inlet in boats covered by a bombardment from land and sea. Brig.-Gen. Alfred H. Terry, with four thousand men, was to make a demonstration on James Island. Col. T. W. Higginson, with part of his First South Carolina Colored and a section of artillery, was to ascend the South Edisto River, and cut the railroad at Jacksonboro. This latter force, however, was repulsed with the loss of two guns and the steamer 'Governor Milton.'"

Unfortunately, the attack was a debacle for the Union, with nearly 350 casualties incurred in the failed attack. The Confederate defenders lost just 12 casualties. Strong described the advance against the fort: "The two columns now moved forward, under a lively discharge of shell, grape, and canister, converging toward the works nearest the southern extremity of the island, and thence along its commanding ridge and eastern coast, capturing successively the eight batteries, of one heavy gun each, occupying the commanding points of that ridge, besides two batteries, mounting, together, three 10-inch seacoast mortars." However, while advancing through fog on the dawn of the 11th, the attack was sharply repulsed by the defenders in the fort, and Gillmore had to go back to the drawing board.

In the days leading up to the second assault on Fort Wagner, the 54th was posted on James Island, where it sought to defend advanced Union positions on that critical island while Confederate forces were also still on it. Eventually, the Union forces withdrew after light skirmishing and retreated back to Folly Island on the 17th. That night, the 54th received orders to embark back to Morris Island and report to General Strong. Emilio described the scene:

"In the evening a moist cool breeze came; and at eight o'clock the regiment moved up the shore to a creek in readiness to embark on the 'General Hunter,' lying in the stream. It was found that the only means of boarding the steamer was by a leaky long-boat which would hold about thirty men. Definite orders came to report the regiment to General Strong at Morris Island without delay, and at 10 P. M. the embarkation began. By the light of a single lantern the men were stowed in the boat.

Rain was pouring down in torrents, for a thunderstorm was raging. Throughout that interminable night the long-boat was kept plying from shore to vessel and back, while those on land stood or crouched about in dripping clothes, awaiting their turn for ferriage to the steamer, whose dim light showed feebly in the gloom. The boat journey was made with difficulty, for the current was strong, and the crowded soldiers obstructed the rowers in their task. It was an all night's work. Colonel Shaw saw personally to the embarkation; and as daylight was breaking he stepped in with the last boat-load, and himself guided the craft to the 'Hunter.' Thus with rare self-sacrifice and fine example, he shared the exposure of every man, when the comfortable cabin of the steamer was at his disposal from the evening before.

On the 'General Hunter' the officers procured breakfast; but the men were still without rations. Refreshed, the officers were all together for the last time socially; before another day three were dead, and three wounded who never returned. Captain Simpkins, whose manly appearance and clear-cut features were so pleasing to look upon, was, as always, quiet and dignified; Captain Russel was voluble and active as ever, despite all fatigue. Neither appeared to have any premonition of their fate. It was different with Colonel Shaw, who again expressed to Lieutenant-Colonel Hallowell his apprehension of speedy death."

On July 18, Gillmore had another assault planned on Fort Wagner. After executing a diversionary attack at Grimball's Landing on July 16, he had ordered an artillery bombardment of the fort, hoping to catch them off-guard. After that, the 54th would be ordered to assault the fort sometime during the early evening.

For most of that late morning and afternoon, there was an artillery exchange between the two sides, and Emilio described it as the 54th awaited its turn: "About 10 A. M., on the 18th, five wooden gunboats joined the land batteries in shelling Wagner, lying out of the enemy's range. At about 12.30 P. M., five monitors and the 'New Ironsides' opened, and the land batteries increased their fire. A deluge of shot was now poured into the work, driving the main portion of its garrison into the bombproofs, and throwing showers of sand from the slopes of Wagner into the air but to fall back in place again. The enemy's flag was twice shot away, and, until replaced, a battle-flag was planted with great gallantry by daring men. From Gregg, Sumter, and the James Island and Sullivan's Island batteries, the enemy returned the iron compliments; while for a time Wagner's cannoneers ran out at intervals, and served a part of the guns, at great risk."

Unfortunately for the Union, the bombardment was doing little damage to the defenders, and only about 20 Confederates were casualties. Furthermore, the garrison's commander, William Taliaferro, realized that the cannonade was a prelude to an infantry assault, so he had his men ready when the artillery stopped. In addition to having soldiers manning the parapets of the fort, a couple companies of soldiers were posted outside of the fort as well.

On the evening of July 18, 1863, the men of the 54th Massachusetts Volunteer Infantry stood watching the sun set over the horizon, awaiting the signal to charge. Tired, hungry, and anxious to prove themselves, they listened as the air filled with the rumble of artillery and could feel the ground trembling beneath their feet. The regiment was to spearhead an assault around dusk, attacking from the west while soldiers under Union General Crockett Strong and Colonel Haldimand S. Putnam attacked the seaward salient on the southern face. Despite how tired out they were from their night passage to Morris Island, Shaw was so eager to have his men participate in the assault that he happily volunteered them for the mission. The 54th would be making an attack that night despite not having eaten since the morning. General Truman Seymour, who would lead the assault, explained why he chose the 54th to spearhead the attack in saying, "It was believed that the Fifty-fourth was in every respect as efficient as any other body of men; and as it was one of the strongest and best officered, there seemed to be no good reason why it should not be selected for the advance. This point was decided by General Strong and myself."

Emilio relayed the tense moments the 54th faced before beginning the assault:

"Away over the sea to the eastward the heavy sea-fog was gathering, the western sky bright with the reflected light, for the sun had set. Far away thunder mingled with the occasional boom of cannon. The gathering host all about, the silent lines stretching away to the rear, the passing of a horseman now and then carrying orders,—all was ominous of the impending onslaught. Far and indistinct in front was the now silent earthwork, seamed, scarred, and ploughed with shot, its flag still waving in defiance.

Among the dark soldiers who were to lead veteran regiments which were equal in drill and discipline to any in the country, there was a lack of their usual lightheartedness, for they realized, partially at least, the dangers they were to encounter. But there was little nervousness and no depression observable. It took but a touch to bring out their irrepressible spirit and humor in the old way. When a cannon-shot from the enemy came toward the line and passed over, a man or two moved nervously, calling out a sharp reproof from Lieutenant-Colonel Hallowell, whom the men still spoke of as 'the major.' Thereupon one soldier quietly remarked to his comrades, 'I guess the major forgets what kind of balls them is!' Another added, thinking of the foe, 'I guess they kind of 'spec's we're coming!'"

Just before the assault, Strong addressed the regiment, telling them, "Boys, I am a Massachusetts man, and I know you will fight for the honor of the State. I am sorry you must go into the fight tired and hungry, but the men in the fort are tired too. There are but three hundred behind those walls, and they have been fighting all day. Don't fire a musket on the way up, but go in and bayonet them at their guns." Shaw simply told them, "Now I want you to prove yourselves men,"

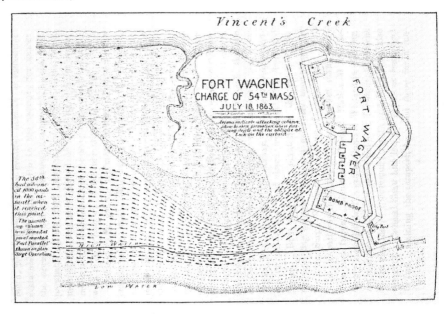

The manner in which the 54th assaulted the fort. The map shows the way the terrain restricted their movements.

Around 7:45, Colonel Shaw, who was walking along the line, moved to the center and commanded his regiment, "Attention!" The regiment then sprang to their feet and began moving forward, heeding Shaw's command, "Move in quick time until within a hundred yards of the fort; then double quick, and charge!" While batteries from nearby Confederate forts started firing shells, some of the men on the right had to march in water up to their knees. Once the 54th was within about 200 yards of the fort, the Confederate defenders opened fire with cannon and muskets, ripping through the regiment's ranks. Emilio described the sights and sounds of the horror:

"At that moment Wagner became a mound of fire, from which poured a stream of shot and shell. Just a brief lull, and the deafening explosions of cannon were renewed, mingled with the crash, and rattle of musketry. A sheet of flame, followed by a running fire, like electric sparks, swept along the parapet, as the Fifty-first North Carolina gave a direct, and the Charleston Battalion a left-oblique, fire on the Fifty-fourth. Their Thirty-first North Carolina had lost heart, and failed to take position in the southeast bastion,—fortunately, too, for had its musketry fire been added to that delivered, it is doubtful whether any Federal troops could have passed the defile.

When this tempest of war came, before which men fell in numbers on every side, the only response the Fifty-fourth made to the deadly challenge was to change step to the double-quick, that it might the sooner close with the foe. There had been no stop, pause, or check at any period of the advance, nor was there now. As the swifter pace was taken, and officers sprang to the fore with waving swords barely seen in the darkness, the men closed the gaps, and with set jaws, panting breath, and bowed heads, charged on.

Wagner's wall, momentarily lit up by cannon-flashes, was still the goal toward which the survivors rushed in sadly diminished numbers. It was now dark, the gloom made more intense by the blinding explosions in the front. This terrible fire which the regiment had just faced, probably caused the greatest number of casualties sustained by the Fifty-fourth in the assault; for nearer the work the men were somewhat sheltered by the high parapet. Every flash showed the ground dotted with men of the regiment, killed or wounded. Great holes, made by the huge shells of the navy or the land batteries, were pitfalls into which the men stumbled or fell."

With their comrades dropping at their feet, the regiment moved forward at the double quick until they finally managed to reach the parapet, where a fierce hand-to-hand struggle ensued. Unfortunately for the 54th, its superiors had woefully underestimated the number of Confederate defenders, which numbered over 1,000. It's estimated the 54th had only about 600 effectives for the attack.

Emilio described the climax of the 54th's assault:

"In the pathway from the defile to the fort many brave men had fallen. Lieutenant-Colonel Hallowell was severely wounded in the groin, Captain Willard in the leg, Adjutant James in the ankle and side, Lieutenant Homans in the shoulder. Lieutenants Smith and Pratt were also wounded. Colonel Shaw had led his regiment from first to last. Gaining the rampart, he stood there for a moment with uplifted sword, shouting, 'Forward, Fifty-fourth!' and then fell dead, shot through the heart, besides other wounds.

Not a shot had been fired by the regiment up to this time. As the crest was gained, the crack of revolver shots was heard, for the officers fired into the surging mass of upturned faces confronting them, lit up redly but a moment by the powder-flashes.

Musket-butts and bayonets were freely used on the parapet, where the stormers were gallantly met. The garrison fought with muskets, handspikes, and gun-rammers, the officers striking with their swords, so close were the combatants. Numbers, however, soon told against the Fifty-fourth, for it was tens against hundreds. Outlined against the sky, they were a fair mark for the foe. Men fell every moment during the brief struggle. Some of the wounded crawled down the slope to shelter; others fell headlong into the ditch below.

It was seen from the volume of musketry fire, even before the walls were gained, that the garrison was stronger than had been supposed, and brave in defending the work. The first rush had failed, for those of the Fifty-fourth who reached the parapet were too few in numbers to overcome the garrison, and the supports were not at hand to take full advantage of their first fierce attack."

One of the 54th's soldiers, George E. Stephens, wrote a letter to Emilio after the war describing the height of the fight:

"I remember distinctly that when our column had charged the fort, passed the half-filled moat, and mounted to the parapet, many of our men clambered over, and some entered by the large embrasure in which one of the big guns was mounted, the firing substantially ceased there by the beach, and the Rebel musketry fire steadily grew hotter on our left. An officer of our regiment called out, 'Spike that gun!' . . . Just at the very hottest moment of the struggle, a battalion or regiment charged up to the moat, halted, and did not attempt to cross it and join us, but from their position commenced to fire upon us. I was one of the men who shouted from where I stood, "Don't fire on us! We are the Fifty-fourth." I have heard it was a Maine regiment. . . . Many of our men will join me in saying that in the early stages of the fight we had possession of the sea end of Battery Wagner. . . . When we reached the Gatling battery drawn up to repel a counter-attack, I remember you were the only commissioned officer present, and you placed us indiscriminately,—that is, without any regard to companies in line,—and proposed to renew the charge. The commanding officer, whom I do not know, ordered us to the flanking rifle-pits, and we then awaited the expected counter-charge the enemy did not make."

As the Union assault quickly disintegrated, Confederate Brigadier General Taliaferro was reinforced by the Thirty-Second Georgia Infantry, which had been transported to the island by Brigadier General Johnson Hagood. The fresh troops swept over the fortress, killing and capturing the remainder of the Union troops, including members of the 54th.

In all, over 1500 Union soldiers were killed, captured, or wounded in the assault, and the Confederates suffered less than 200 casualties. Only 350 men of the 54th were still standing by the time they had retreated. They had lost 30 killed in action, 24 mortally wounded, 15 captured, and over 50 missing. The regiment had lost several officers, including Colonel Shaw and two captains, while every other captain had been injured. In fact, by the time the attack was over, the commanding figure in the regiment was Emilio himself, due to the attrition. He described some of the acts of heroism he saw at the height of the hand-to-hand fighting:

> "One brave fellow, with his broken arm lying across his breast, was piling cartridges upon it for Lieutenant Emerson, who, like other officers, was using a musket he had picked up. Another soldier, tired of the enforced combat, climbed the slope to his fate; for in a moment his dead body rolled down again. A particularly severe fire came from the southwest bastion. There a Confederate was observed, who, stripped to the waist, with daring exposure for some time dealt out fatal shots; but at last three eager marksmen fired together, and he fell back into the fort, to appear no more. Capt. J. W. M. Appleton distinguished himself before the curtain. He crawled into an embrasure, and with his pistol prevented the artillery-men from serving the gun. Private George Wilson of Company A had been shot through both shoulders, but refused to go back until he had his captain's permission. While occupied with this faithful soldier, who came to him as he lay in the embrasure, Captain Appleton's attention was distracted, and the gun was fired.
>
> In the fighting upon the slopes of Wagner, Captains Russel and Simpkins were killed or mortally wounded. Captain Pope there received a severe wound in the shoulder."

Soon after the Battle of Fort Wagner, the actions of Sergeant William H. Carney, a non-commissioned black officer of the 54th, spread across the country. As the heroic story unfolded, it became known that during the battle, Carney, who was studying to be a minister when he decided the best way to serve his Lord and help his people would be to join the Union, had witnessed the company flag-bearer fall wounded. Before the flag could even fall to the ground, Sergeant Carney took the flag from the wounded soldier and was hit by several bullets as he ran. When a soldier from another regiment offered to take the flag so that Carney could seek medical attention, Carney replied, "No one but a member of the 54th should carry the colors!"[5] Upon carrying the flag back into camp after the battle, he received rousing cheers from the other units, and he sang, "Boys, the old flag never touched the ground!" Three decades later, when he received the Congressional Medal of Honor for his exceptional bravery, he said, "I only did my duty." Although other black soldiers were awarded the Medal of Honor prior to Carney receiving his, Carney's is the earliest documented action for which the Medal of Honor was awarded to an African American.

---

[5] Civil War Trust website: Civil War.org, "Fort Wagner and the 54th Massachusetts Volunteer Infantry."

Carney

Rick Reeves' painting, *The Old Flag Never Touched the Ground*

There was controversy over what happened to Shaw's body after the battle, and one Confederate officer claimed,

"Colonel Shaw fell on the left of our flagstaff about ten yards towards the river, near the bombproof immediately on our works, with a number of his officers and men. He was instantly killed, and fell outside of our works. The morning following the battle his body was carried through our lines; and I noticed that he was stripped of all his clothing save under-vest and drawers. This desecration of the dead we endeavored to provide against; but at that time— the incipiency of the Rebellion—our men were so frenzied that it was next to impossible to guard against it; this desecration, however, was almost exclusively participated in by the more desperate and lower class of our troops. Colonel Shaw's body was brought in from the sally-port on the Confederate right, and conveyed across the parade-ground into the bombproof by four of our men of the burial party. Soon after, his body was carried out via the sally-port on the left river-front, and conveyed across the front of our works, and there buried. . . . His watch and chain were robbed from his body by a private in my company, by name Charles Blake. I think he had other personal property of Colonel Shaw. . . . Blake, with other members of my company, jumped our works at night after hostilities had ceased, and robbed the dead. . . . Colonel Shaw was the only officer buried with the colored troops. . . ."

Burying Shaw's boy like that outraged the North, since his body could have very easily been transferred back to Union lines. As Emilio noted, "Such disposal of the remains of an officer of Colonel Shaw's rank, when his friends were almost within call, was so unusual and cruel that there seemed good ground for the belief that the disposition made was so specially directed, as a premeditated indignity for having dared to lead colored troops. When known throughout the North, it excited general indignation, and fostered bitterness."

When the Union later occupied Morris Island near the end of the war, Robert's father Francis wrote to Gillmore asking them not to try to dig up his son's grave, telling the general, "I take the liberty to address you because I am informed that efforts are to be made to recover the body of my son, Colonel Shaw of the Fifty-fourth Massachusetts Regiment, which was buried at Fort Wagner. My object in writing is to say that such efforts are not authorized by me or any of my family, and that they are not approved by us. We hold that a soldier's most appropriate burial-place is on the field where he has fallen. I shall therefore be much obliged, General, if in case the matter is brought to your cognizance, you will forbid the desecration of my son's grave, and prevent the disturbance of his remains or those buried with him. With most earnest wishes for your success, I am, sir, with respect and esteem,"

Though the Second Battle of Fort Wagner was a decisive defeat for the Union, it proved that black soldiers could fight just as hard as their white counterparts. Furthermore, the battle brought significant glory to the 54th, which helped spur additional recruitment of black soldiers. At the same time, however, now that black troops were being used and captured in war, the issue of how the Confederates dealt with them as prisoners became a national issue. The South had already made clear that they intended to punish white officers with death for inciting slave insurrections if they led black soldiers, and black soldiers knew they would fare no better. On July 18, the very same date as the attack on Fort Wagner, a Charleston publication reported:

"Fourteen blacks fell into our hands, including a sergeant and corporal. Five claimed to be free, the remainder finally confessing they were runaway slaves. One hailed from Michigan, two or three from Massachusetts, one from Missouri, one from Maryland, and several from Kentucky. One rascal, running up with his musket, exclaimed, 'Here, mossa, nebber shoot him off—tak um!' showing evidently his low country origin, but unfortunately somebody's gun went off about the same time, and the fellow was killed. They received no tender treatment during the skirmish, and the marsh in one place was thick with their dead bodies. . . . The prisoners believe they are to be hung, and give for a reason for fighting as well as they did, that they would rather die of bullet than rope. It is a nice question whether they are to be recognized as belligerents or outlaws; and the indignation of our troops is not concealed at the thought that a white man may, by virtue of these captures, be one day exchanged for a negro. The suggestion I have heard on the subject is that we may be compelled to respect the free blacks as recognized citizens of the North taken in arms, but that when a runaway slave is recaptured, he should be turned over to his master, and by him to the civil authorities, to be disposed of according to law."

By the end of July, President Lincoln had to announce his own policy in an effort to ensure captured black soldiers were treated like captured white soldiers:

"Executive mansion, Washington, July 30, 1863.

It is the duty of every government to give protection to its citizens of whatever class, color, or condition, and especially to those who are duly organized as soldiers in the public service. The law of nations and the usages and customs of war, as carried on by civilized powers, permit no distinction as to color in the treatment of prisoners of war as public enemies. To sell or enslave any captured person on account of his color, and for no offence against the laws of war, is a relapse into barbarism and a crime against the civilization of the age. The Government of the United States will give the same protection to all its soldiers; and if the enemy shall sell or enslave any one because of his color, the offence shall be punished by retaliation upon the enemy's prisoners in our hands.

It is therefore ordered that for every soldier of the United States killed in violation of the laws of war, a Rebel soldier shall be executed, and for every one enslaved by the enemy or sold into slavery, a Rebel soldier shall be placed at hard labor on the public works, and continue at such labor until the other shall be released and receive the treatment due a prisoner of war.

Abraham Lincoln.

By order of the Secretary of War, E. D. Townsend, Assistant Adjutant-General."

After the war, when the horrors of POW camps like Andersonville were exposed, the full extent of just how poorly Union prisoners were treated became public. It was even worse for black soldiers, as Emilio noted:

Stripped of necessary clothing, robbed of their valuables and of priceless mementos, the unfortunate captives, often wounded, were marched for miles over the roads or crowded like cattle into cars that bore them to this or that prison pen. Shrinking with horror at the sight of the terrible misery which met their eyes, they were thrust into the midst of the inferno from which in most cases they were only to emerge as corpses or physical wrecks throughout the remainder of life. Starved, left to dig into the ground for shelter like wild beasts, maltreated, reviled, shot at if in misery or diseased mind they wandered to the dead-line, reeking in filth, covered with vermin, shaking with fever or cold, stricken with scurvy, the hapless victims lived on as best they could, but to endure until hope of release grew faint with waning strength, while their captors strove to sap their loyalty by offers of freedom, would they but enlist in their ranks, or labor on their works."

Ironically, around the very time the 54th would be used in the attack on Fort Wagner, simmering racial discord climaxed during the New York Draft Riots, the largest civil insurrection in American history. From July 13-16, 1863, violent disturbances erupted in New York City, the culmination of working-class discontent with new laws passed by Congress that year to draft men to fight in the Civil War. During the riots, African Americans along the city's waterfront and Lower East Side were beaten, tortured, and lynched by mobs angry about conscription and scapegoating blacks for being the cause of the war. Though intended to express anger at the draft, the protests turned horribly violent, and at least 100 African Americans were ultimately killed

By the time Major General John E. Wool, commander of the Department of the East, reached the scene, mobs had already ransacked or destroyed numerous buildings, including the homes of abolitionists and known abolitionist sympathizers, many African Americans' homes, and even the Colored Orphan Asylum at 44th Street and Fifth Avenue. In the aftermath, many whites admitted that they had directed their frustration toward blacks because they felt that the Civil War was ultimately caused by them.

Chapter 6: Florida

For the remainder of 1863, the 54th participated in siege operations around Charleston before boarding transports for Florida early in February of 1864. The regiment, now numbering just over 500 men, the rest having been detailed for other duty, was now led by Colonel Edward Hallowell, who had succeeded Shaw. Anxious to avenge the Fort Wagner repulse, the 54th Massachusetts Volunteer Infantry was made available to Brigadier General Truman Seymour, the Union commander of the Florida Expedition.

Edward Hallowell

In February 1864, Major General Quincy A. Gillmore, commander of the Union's Department of the South at Hilton Head, South Carolina, ordered Brigadier General Seymour to launch an expedition into Florida to secure Union enclaves, sever Confederate supply routes, and recruit additional black soldiers by taking in escaped slaves. Landing at Jacksonville, Seymour's forces made several raids into northeast and north-central Florida, meeting little resistance while seizing several Confederate camps, capturing small Confederate units and artillery pieces, and liberating slaves, who they invited into their ranks. Meanwhile, Confederate General P. G. T. Beauregard felt that the Union presence in Florida posed enough of a threat to detach reinforcements under Major General Alfred H. Colquitt to stop Seymour.

Seymour, disregarding direct orders from Gillmore not to advance deep into the state, began a drive across northern Florida bent on capturing Tallahassee. Following the Florida, Atlantic and Gulf Central Railroad line, Seymour led his 5,500 men in the direction of Lake City, in Columbia County. On the afternoon of February 20, Seymour encountered Confederate General Joseph Finegan's 5,000 troops near Olustee Station in Baker County, and Finegan dispatched an infantry brigade to meet Seymour's advance units and to lure them into the Confederate entrenchments. Assuming that he was once again facing the same Florida militia units he had previously routed with relative ease, Finnegan committed his troops tentatively instead of mounting a concerted offensive. Finally meeting at Ocean Pond, a battle ensued in open pine woods, with both Finegan and Seymour reinforcing their engaged units throughout the course of the afternoon.

With the battle raging on throughout the afternoon, Finegan finally committed the last of his reserves, causing the Union line to break and forcing a retreat, but he did not exploit the withdrawal, allowing most of the fleeing Union forces to reach Jacksonville unmolested. Launching a last-ditch attempt to engage the rear units of Seymour's forces just before nightfall, the Confederates were handily repulsed by men from the 54th, as well as soldiers from the 34th U.S. Colored Troops. Emilio described the fighting:

This spirited movement into action of the colored brigade is acknowledged to have caused the enemy's right to give way somewhat, and imperilled the guns of Captain Wheaton's Chatham Artillery. Under cover of its onset Seymour withdrew his white troops to a new line some one hundred yards in the rear,—Langdon being forced to abandon three of his guns. This retirement was continued in successive lines of battle. A newspaper correspondent, writing of the action, said, 'The two colored regiments had stood in the gap and saved the army.' But the cost had been great, particularly to the First North Carolina, for it lost Lieut.-Col. Wm. N. Reed, commanding, mortally wounded; Maj. A. Bogle, Adjt. W. C. Manning, three captains, and five lieutenants wounded; one captain killed, and some two hundred and thirty enlisted men killed, wounded, or missing. Having maintained the contest for some time, it was withdrawn.

Every organization had retired but the Fifty-fourth, and our regiment stood alone. From the position first taken up it still held back the enemy in its front. What had occurred elsewhere was not known."

Lithograph depicting black soldiers at the Battle of Olustee

Although the 54th had repulsed that final attack, the Battle of Olustee is still considered a debacle for the Union, which lost nearly 2000 soldiers due to the insubordination of its commanding officer. In the aftermath of the Battle of Olustee, the men of the 54th Massachusetts physically pulled a trainload of wounded Union soldiers five miles along the tracks until horses could be secured to transport them further. This story of bravery, effectiveness, and sheer brute strength spread across the North, earning the regiment more acclaim.

Chapter 7: Back to South Carolina

After Olustee, the 54th would be sent back to South Carolina, to the very same area where their fateful attack on Fort Wagner had taken place. Meanwhile, the issue of unequal pay had forced their leader, Hallowell, to actually leave the regiment and lobby for equal pay in the North. Despite having been assured equal treatment, white soldiers were paid $13 a month with nothing withheld for clothing, while the men of the 54th were paid $10 a month and had $3 withheld for clothes. Although the government of Massachusetts offered to cover the difference, it was a personal issue for the men, and they began boycotting their payments. In fact, at Olustee, they moved forward shouting, "Massachusetts and Seven Dollars a Month!" Around that same time, Congress finally relented, passing a bill ordering equal pay for black soldiers.

Leaving Hilton Head on November 28, 1864 for Boyd's Neck, Union General John P. Hatch set out with orders to cut off the Charleston and Savannah Railroad in support of Sherman's March to the Sea, which was projected to arrive near Savannah at some point near the end of 1864. Leading a compliment of 5,000 men, including two brigades of the Coast Division of the Department of the South, one naval brigade, and portions of three batteries of light artillery, Hatch and his troops steamed up the Broad River in transports intending to interrupt the Charleston and Savannah Railroad near Pocotaligo, only to find that their maps and guides were inaccurate.

Hatch was unable to actually proceed on the correct route until the morning of November 30, and near Honey Hill, the men encountered a Confederate force of regulars and militia under the command of Colonel Charles J. Colcock, with a battery of seven guns across the road. Sending in the 54th and 55th Massachusetts under Colonel Alfred S. Hartwell to engage the enemy, it soon became apparent that the positioning of the Union forces was such that only one section of artillery could be used at a time, and that Confederate troops were too well embedded to be dislodged. Emilio described the fighting:

"Our advance had crossed the field, when, at 8.30 A. M.,, the first cannon-shot was heard, coming from the enemy. General Hatch formed line of battle, and Lieut. E. A. Wildt's section, Battery B, Third New York, shelled the Confederates. Then our skirmishers entered the woods and Col. George W. Baird's Thirty-second United States. Colored Troops, moving along the causeway by the flank at the double-quick, through a severe fire which wounded Lieut.-Col. Edward C. Geary and killed or wounded a number of men, cleared the head of the causeway. Before this retirement the enemy set fire to the dead grass and stubble of an old field beyond the swamp which delayed our progress as intended, and they continued to annoy our advance with occasional shots. Over part of the way still farther onward the troops were confined to the narrow road in column by woods and swamps, while the skirmishers and flankers struggled through vines and underbrush. At a point where the road turned to the left, Colcock made his last stand before seeking his works at Honey Hill; and in the artillery firing that ensued the brave Lieutenant Wildt received a mortal wound.

Colonel Hartwell, commanding the Second Brigade, with eight companies of the Fifty-fifth Massachusetts under Lieut.-Col. Charles B. Fox, hearing volley firing breaking the pervading stillness, moved rapidly to the front. There the leaders filing along the wood-road, three companies became separated from the regiment when Colonel Hartwell ordered a charge in double column. Twice forced to fall back by the enemy's fire, their brave colonel giving the command, 'Follow your colors!' and himself leading on horseback, the Fifty-fifth turned the bend, rushed up the road, and in the face of a deadly fire advanced to the creek. But it was fruitless, for the pitiless shot and shell so decimated the ranks that the survivors retired after losing over one hundred men in five minutes, including Color Sergeant King, killed, and Sergeant-Major Trotter, Sergeant Shorter, and Sergeant Mitchell, wounded. Colonel Hartwell, wounded and pinned to the ground by his dead horse, was rescued and dragged to the wood by the gallant Lieut. Thomas F. Ellsworth of his regiment. Captains Crane and Boynton were both killed after displaying fearless gallantry. The One Hundred and Twenty-seventh New York supported this charge by an advance, but after the repulse retired also."

Fighting until dark, Hatch finally conceded the futility of further attacks and withdrew back to his transports. Nearly 100 Union soldiers, mostly black, were killed, and over 600 wounded. In the aftermath, commanding officer Brigadier General Potter said about the black soldiers: "I cannot close this report without making honorable mention of the good conduct and steadiness displayed by the officers and men under the most trying circumstances. Exposed to a heavy fire from a concealed enemy who was strongly entrenched, and laboring under every disadvantage of ground, they maintained their position with the greatest tenacity and endurance. Nothing but the formidable character of the obstacles they encountered prevented them from achieving success."[6]

Chapter 8: Battle of Boykin's Mill

The location of the final battle of the Civil War on South Carolina soil, as well as the last Union officer killed in action, Boykin's Mill was also the last pitched combat for the 54th. Under orders to disable railroads in South Carolina, Potter's brigades were forced to first contend with the First Kentucky Mounted Infantry Brigade from April 9, 1865, the same day Lee was surrendering to Grant at Appomattox, until April 18, when they reengaged in the quiet town of Boykin, South Carolina. At the ensuing Battle of Boykin's Mill, the Confederates held a strong defensive position in an abandoned fort that provided only a single-file assault on their stronghold. Tasked with leading the charge, the 54th Massachusetts was so fierce in their attack that Confederate troops ran from the field, but not before two black infantrymen were killed and 13 wounded. The two killed were Corporal James P. Johnson and Lieutenant E. L. Stevens, the latter having the distinction of being the last Union officer killed in action during the Civil War.

After an unsuccessful attempt to catch the fleeing Confederates, Union troops burned the mill to the ground, based on General Sherman's scorched earth policy. The Battle of Boykin's Mill proved to be the bloodiest battle of the South Carolina Campaign for the 54th, and the regiment suffered the highest casualty rate of Potter's raid.

Although the preliminary cessation of hostilities was announced to both sides two days later on April 21, and Confederate Army of Northern Virginia commander Robert E Lee had surrendered at Appomattox Court House on April 9, 1865, Confederate General Joseph E. Johnston did not officially surrender the men in his department to General Sherman until April 29.

Fittingly, at the conclusion of the war, the 54th was stationed in none other than Charleston, one of the first hotbeds of secession and the city that the 54th had spent much of its Civil War service trying to capture. Emilio recalled the Independence Day celebrations in the city in 1865:

---

[6] DCNYHistory.org website, "Report of Brigadier General Edward E. Potter, U. S. Army, Commanding First Brigade."

"Independence Day was celebrated with great enthusiasm by the loyal citizens and soldiery. National salutes were fired from Sumter, Moultrie, Bee, Wagner, and Gregg, the harbor resounding with explosions, bringing to memory the days of siege. The troops paraded, the Declaration of Independence and the Emancipation Proclamation were read, and orators gave expression to patriotic sentiments doubly pointed by the great war which perfected the work of the fathers."

A week later, the 54th was officially mustered out of service.

Chapter 9: The Legacy of the 54th Massachusetts

Due to the extraordinary circumstances of their military involvement in the Civil War, and the precedent it set, the 54th Massachusetts Volunteer Infantry Regiment became one of the most famous regiments of the entire Civil War. Though it was not involved in a great number of battles during its twenty-seven-month commission, the bravery of its officers and soldiers at Fort Wagner, Olustee and Honey Hill truly did earn them honor and glory. Of the men originally mustered into the 54th, more than a third of them were killed or wounded in combat, an incredibly high casualty rate that speaks to their courage and steadfastness. As Emilio put it:

In connection with other colored organizations, the Fifty-fourth contributed to the establishment of a fact bearing strongly upon the military resources of our country then and now. We have read in the opening chapter that the United States only called the blacks to bear arms when disaster covered the land with discouragement and volunteering had ceased. It is also to be remembered that our enemy, having from the incipiency of the Rebellion employed this class as laborers for warlike purposes, at the last resolved upon enrolling them in their armies. This plan, however, was still-born, and was the final and wildest dream of Davis, Lee, and the crumbling Confederacy. But the courage and fidelity of the blacks, so unmistakably demonstrated during the Civil War, assures to us, in the event of future need, a class to recruit from now more available, intelligent, educated, and self-reliant, and more patriotic, devoted, and self-sacrificing, if such were possible, than thirty years ago."

In a large sense, the 54th's greatest legacy was the manner in which they served as a vanguard for further participation in the war by black soldiers. By the end of the Civil War, an estimated 180,000 black men served in the Army, an estimated 10% of all soldiers, and nearly 20,000 served in the Navy. Black soldiers served in the artillery and infantry, in addition to performing all the noncombat duties needed to sustain an army. Additionally, African Americans contributed to the war effort as carpenters, laborers, chaplains, cooks, scouts, guards, nurses, spies, steamboat pilots, teamsters, and surgeons. Black women who could not formally join the Army served as nurses, spies, and scouts, the most famous being Harriet Tubman, who scouted for the Second South Carolina Volunteers. By the end of the war, there were nearly 80 commissioned officers who were black, and 40,000 black soldiers died during the war.

Nevertheless, as the experiences of the 54th demonstrated, ongoing racial prejudice ensured that black soldiers were not used in combat during the Civil War as extensively as they might have been. A considerable number of whites didn't trust them and sometimes preferred to face an enemy against the odds rather than fight side-by-side with them. Nevertheless, black soldiers served with distinction and honor in a number of battles, including Milliken's Bend and Port Hudson in Louisiana, the Battle of the Crater during the Siege of Petersburg in Virginia, and in Nashville. Of course, at the top of the list was the 54th's assault on Fort Wagner, in which the regiment's casualties included two-thirds of their officers and half their troops. In all, 16 black soldiers were ultimately awarded the Congressional Medal of Honor for their extraordinary valor.

In addition to fighting just as nobly, black soldiers also faced far greater peril when captured by the Confederate Army. Although the Lincoln Administration's threat to execute Confederate prisoners if they mistreated black soldiers generally restrained the South, black soldiers were still threatened with being forced into slavery. Furthermore, Confederates sometimes refused to give black soldiers quarter at all, and the most controversial battle of the entire war took place at the Battle of Fort Pillow, when Nathan Bedford Forrest's Confederates were accused of massacring the Union garrison, much of which consisted of black soldiers, after they had surrendered. Though Forrest denied the accusations of a massacre, he claimed that the black soldiers were runaway slaves and taunted his men beforehand. A *New York Times* article published at the time of Forrest's death stated, "It is in connection with one of the most atrocious and cold-blooded massacres that ever disgraced civilized warfare that his name will forever be inseparably associated. 'Fort Pillow Forrest' was the title which the deed conferred upon him, and by this he will be remembered by the present generation, and by it he will pass into history."[7]

Without question, the men of the 54th had fought for themselves, but they also fought for a cause, and the Union's victory made it possible. Once the Civil War was over, slavery was made illegal throughout the United States with the adoption of the 13th Amendment, passed by the Senate on April 8, 1864, by the House on January 31, 1865, and adopted on December 6, 1865.

Over the last 150 years, the 54th has remained a popularly remembered Civil War regiment, especially in Massachusetts. A monument constructed between 1884–1898 by renowned sculptor and monument builder Augustus Saint-Gaudens on the Boston Common is part of the *Boston Black Heritage Trail*. Commemorating Robert Gould Shaw and his men, the monument is part of a trail that begins at the Abiel Smith School at 46 Joy Street, which houses the Museum of African American History. The trail also includes the renowned African Meeting House, the first African-American church in the United States, which was built in 1806 at 8 Smith Court and was the site of many speeches given by Frederick Douglass, including his impassioned calls for blacks to take up arms against the South during the Civil War.

---

[7] *New York Times* Article Index website.

In the musical composition, "Col. Shaw and his Colored Regiment," written by world-renowned composer Charles Ives, the opening movement of *Three Places in New England*, is based on both Saint-Gaudens' monument and the famous regiment.

Colonel Shaw and his Black regiment are also featured prominently in Robert Lowell's Civil War Centennial poem, "For the Union Dead" (1964):

> *He is out of bounds now. He rejoices in man's lovely,*
> *peculiar power to choose life and die*
> *when he leads his black soldiers to death,*
> *he cannot bend his back . . .*

Shaw's memory has been immortalized in that manner, but his remains were never moved from Morris Island by men. Due to the tides and the position of Fort Wagner, most of it was eroded within the subsequent decades, and along with the fort, the remains of Colonel Shaw and his men were washed out to sea.

More than a century after the Civil War, its most famous black unit garnered new attention and popularity when the blockbuster film *Glory* hit theaters in 1989. Directed by Edward Zwick and starring Matthew Broderick, Denzel Washington, Cary Elwes, and Morgan Freeman (screenplay by Kevin Jarre), the movie recounted the story of the famous regiment, prior to and including the famous bloody battle at Fort Wagner, based on the personal letters of Colonel Robert Gould Shaw and the novels *Lay This Laurel* (by Lincoln Kirstein) and *One Gallant Rush* (by Peter Burchard). The soundtrack, composed by American composer James Horner [*Braveheart, Willow, Apollo 13, Star Trek II: The Wrath of Khan, Cocoon, Legends of the Fall, Aliens, The Mask of Zorro* . . .] in conjunction with the Boys Choir of Harlem, was released on January 23, 1990.

In addition to reintroducing the 54th to entirely new generations of Americans, the film ultimately went on to receive Academy Award nominations for Best Editing and Best Art Direction, and it won a number of awards from the British Academy Awards and the Golden Globes. Denzel Washington won the Academy Award for Best Supporting Actor.

Bibliography

B Company 54th Mass Vol Inf Regiment, Washington, D. C. website: http://54thmass.org/home.html accessed 08.25.2012.

Catton, Bruce. *Grant Takes Command.* New York: Little, Brown and Company, 1968.

Civil War Trust website: Civil War.org, "Fort Wagner and the 54th Massachusetts Volunteer Infantry" accessed via http://www.civilwar.org/battlefields/batterywagner/battery-wagner-history-articles/fortwagnerpohanka.html 08.26.2012.

DCNYHistory.org website, "Report of Brigadier General Edward E. Potter, U.S. Army, Commanding First Brigade" accessed via http://www.dcnyhistory.org/gary/orpotter.html 08.26.2012.

Emilio, Luis F. *A Brave Black Regiment: The History of the Fifty-Fourth Regiment of Massachusetts Volunteer Infantry, 1863-1865*

Klose, Nelson, and Robert F. Jones. *United States History: To 1877*. New York: Barron's, 1994.

Lanning, Michael. *The Civil War 100*. Illinois: Sourcebooks, Inc., 2006.

National Archives website, "Blacks in the Civil War": http://www.archives.gov/education/lessons/blacks-civil-war/ accessed 08.25.2012.

New York Times Article Index website: Accessed via http://www.nytimes.com/ref/membercenter/nytarchive.html 08.26.2012.

PBS.org website, "Slavery and the Making of America": http://www.pbs.org/wnet/slavery/experience/legal/history.html accessed 08.23.2012.

PBS.org website, *Africans in America*, "The Civil War": http://www.pbs.org/wgbh/aia/part4/4narr5.html accessed 08.25.2012.

Stevens, Joseph E. *1863: The Rebirth of a Nation*. New York: Bantam Books, 1999.

Weider History group, History net.com website: http://www.historynet.com/americas-civil-war-54th-massachusetts-regiment.htm accessed 08.22.2012.

Made in the USA
Coppell, TX
15 October 2024

38648774R10026